SOCKS

SOCKS

A Footloose Miscellany for Sock Lovers and Wearers

WENDI AARONS ✕ Illustrated by KADNA ANDA

CHRONICLE BOOKS
SAN FRANCISCO

Library of Congress Cataloging-in-Publication Data available.

ISBN 978-1-7972-1276-0

Manufactured in China.

MIX
Paper | Supporting
responsible forestry
FSC™ C008047
FSC
www.fsc.org

Design by Rachel Harrell.

Crocs is a registered trademark of Crocs Retail, LLC; Instagram is a registered
trademark of Instagram, LLC; LEGO is a registered trademark of Lego Juris A/S
Corporation; SpongeBob is a registered trademark of Viacom International Inc.;
Swarovski is a registered trademark of Swarovski Aktiengesellschaft.

10 9 8 7 6 5 4 3 2 1

Chronicle books and gifts are available at special quantity discounts to corpo-
rations, professional associations, literacy programs, and other organizations.
For details and discount information, please contact our premiums department
at corporatesales@chroniclebooks.com or at 1-800-759-0190.

Chronicle Books LLC
680 Second Street
San Francisco, California 94107
www.chroniclebooks.com

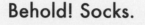

Behold! Socks.

The lowly foot warmer.
The comfortable companion.
The easiest gift on the planet.

What would we do without them?
Probably have cold feet.

You Can Tell a Lot About a Person by the Socks They Wear

It's said the eyes are the window to the soul, but the truth can be found a little lower. Socks are the real window to the sole. If you want to learn all about someone, just take a good gander at what's on their feet.

Wool Socks

Burly. Outdoorsy. Afraid of nothing.
Still likes to keep their tootsies toasty.

Argyle
Socks

Serious. Successful. Has both a favorite
economist and a favorite brand of tea.

Novelty Socks

May be a grown-up, but still wants
to be considered wild and crazy.
At least around the ankles.

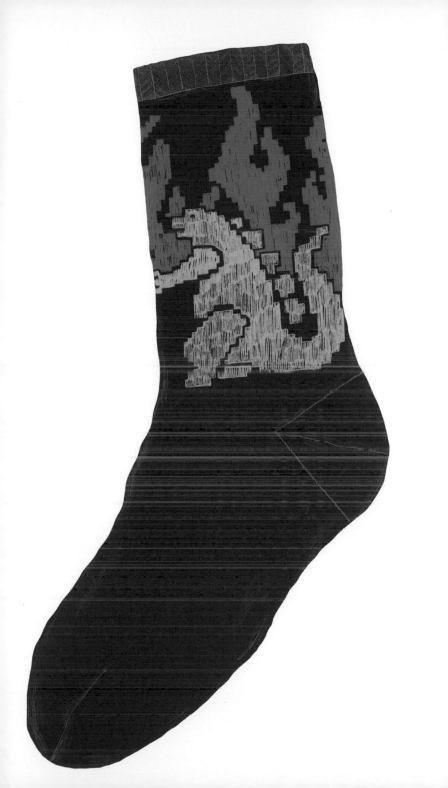

Athletic Socks

Likes to sweat. In socks. That should
then be thrown away because ewww.
Nothing's grosser than sweaty socks.

Dress Socks

Proud owner of three pairs of loafers, three Labradors, and three 401(k)s.

ALTERNATIVE USES
FOR SOCKS:

GET
CRAFTY!

SOCK PUPPET ADVENTURE

Hot glue novelty eyeballs to an old sock, stick
your hand inside, and voila! You now have
another way to annoy your family. Hey, don't
knock it. Shari Lewis made an entire career
out of this shit.

FORT KNOX SOCK

Lots of loose change, but nowhere to stash it?
Simply pour your pennies into a sock, then
seal your new bank account shut with a few zip
ties for added security. When it's time to buy new
socks, you'll know just where to look for the funds.

DIY PRISON WEAPON

It's no fun to be stuck in prison without a handmade weapon. So simply stuff a bar of soap into a sock to make a "slock," then wildly swing it at your gen pop enemies until you become leader of the gang. Sock is the new black.

PATHETIC MITTENS

Don't waste money on fancy leather gloves when there's a cheaper solution. Stick your paws into a pair of socks, and bam! Your hands will stay nice and warm. Then when your feet get cold, do the opposite. Ignore the haters.

BEAN BAGS OF FUN

We all know that America's favorite sport is cornhole. But what if you have a hole and no corn to throw at it? Easy! Fill a sock with beans or rice or anything that falls into the exciting legume category, seal it up with a few staples, and you're ready to rock the backyard BBQ. Hole in one!

COFFEE MUG COZY

"Ewww, is this your old sweat sock?" your partner might ask when they see the cut-up sock covering their favorite mug. "The one you wore to play basketball yesterday? Did you at least wash it first?" Ignore all of that because what they really mean is, "Thank you for this amazing gift. You are a genius."

Mismatched Socks

Says things like, "What? They're both socks. Doesn't that count as matching? I have more important things to worry about, like my carrier pigeons."

No-Show Socks

Wears socks, but doesn't want anyone to know they're wearing them. They're kind of secretive that way. Are they in the witness protection program? They'll never tell.

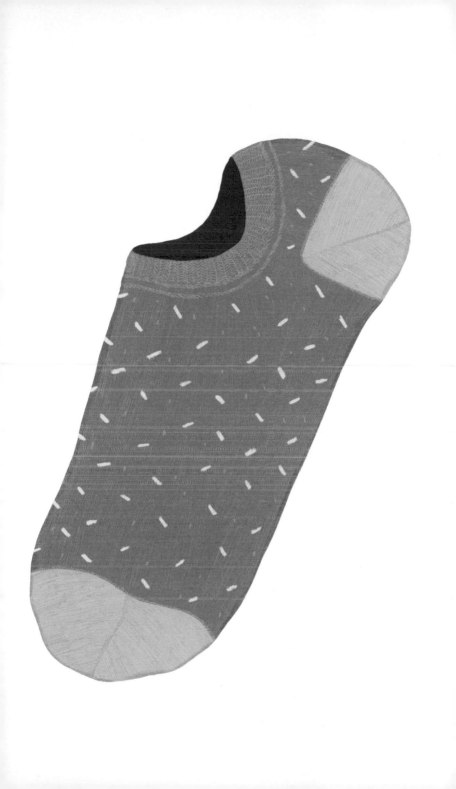

Striped Socks

A bit whimsical. A bit arty. Loves museum gift shops, which is where they bought these socks. Obviously.

Socks with a Hole in One Toe

Are they cheap? A secret exhibitionist? Both? Darn it.

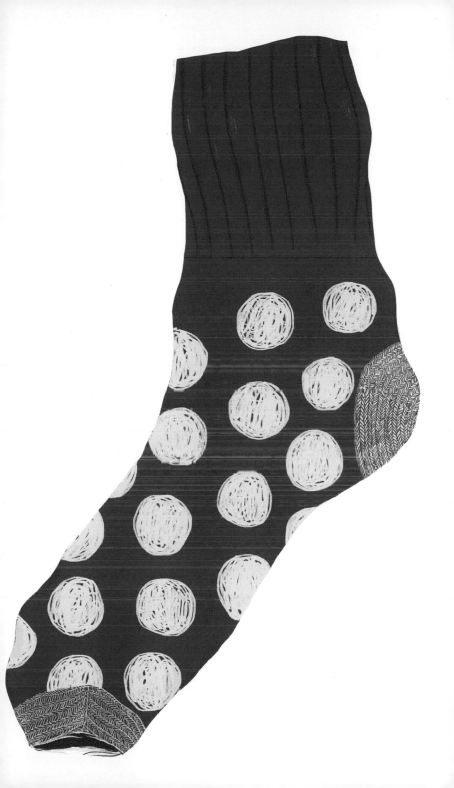

Party Socks

Ain't no party like a fun sock party 'cause a fun sock party don't stop. Until they put their shoes back on. Then the party's over.

FAMOUS SOCKS

THROUGHOUT HISTORY

THE SOCKS NAPOLEON WORE AT THE BATTLE OF WATERLOO
Short. Weak. Fell down midway through.

JAZZ AGE SOCKS
Little known fact: The legendary Cotton Club musicians had a secret group called the Cotton Club Cotton Sock Club. Doo-yah-dah-dah-dit-dip-bah!

AMELIA EARHART'S SOCKS
Good news: not lost in the dryer.
Bad news: lost somewhere over the Atlantic.

JOHNNY CASH'S SOCKS
A sock named Sue. These socks walk the line.
Sometimes they even stepped into a burning ring
of fire. And they were always the same color.
(Hint: It rhymes with "black.")

SOCKS WORN AT WOODSTOCK
Tie-dyed. Covered in mud. Someone probably
tried to smoke them. Likes to say, "You had to be
there, man." Peace.

DISCO SOCKS
The velvet rope didn't keep this glittery pair from
dancing the night away at Studio 54. Even John
Travolta knows that you can't do the Hustle with
bare toes. Toot toot, yeah, beep beep.

Lucky Socks

Wears these every time they buy a lottery ticket or the big game is on. Do not touch the lucky socks. It is bad luck to touch the lucky socks.

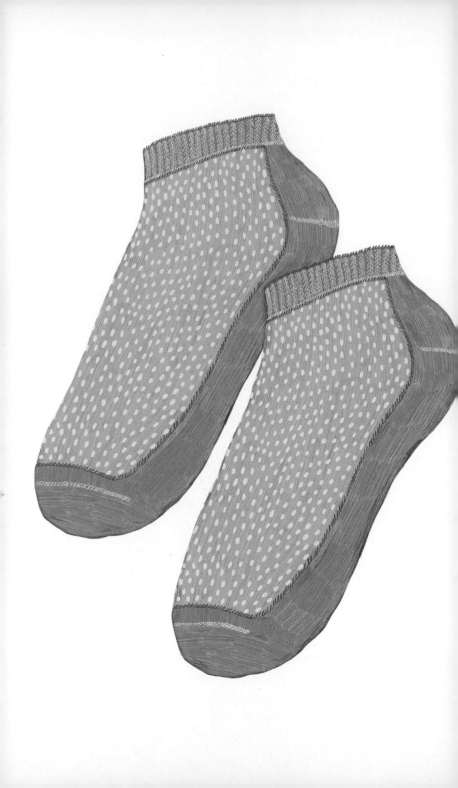

Mesh Socks

A goodfella. Probably has a new TV
to sell you that just "fell off a truck."
Fuhgeddaboudit.

Antimicrobial Socks

They know that bacteria lead to smelly feet,
so they cut those suckers off at the pass.
They're germ free, odor free,
footloose, and fancy-free.

1970s-Style Tube Socks

Fans of these classic socks pull them right up to the knee. As the saying goes, "The higher the sock, the closer to God." Or at least closer to Larry Bird and Dr. J.

Toe Socks

Free spirited. Unconventional. Diet: vegan.
Love: free. Transportation: unicycle.

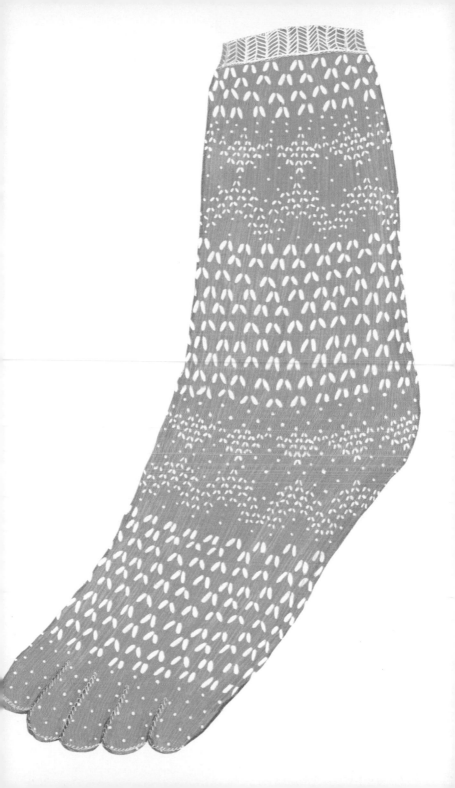

POSTCARDS FROM MISSING SOCKS

So, you're missing a sock. Where did it go? Will it ever come back? Does it miss you as much as you miss it? Or maybe it's now living its best sock life.

Albuquerque New Mexico

It's a dry heat.
Like in the dryer where
you last saw me.

Yosemite National Park

Camping is great.
I'm my own sleeping bag!

IF I CAN MAKE IT
HERE, I CAN MAKE
IT ANYWHERE

NEW YORK CITY

Low-Cut Socks

Likes to show a lot of leg.
Why keep those stems under wraps?
If you've got it, flaunt it, baby.

Black Socks with Sandals

Only wears this combo on two occasions: mowing the lawn and meeting their children's fiancé(e)s. A true classic.

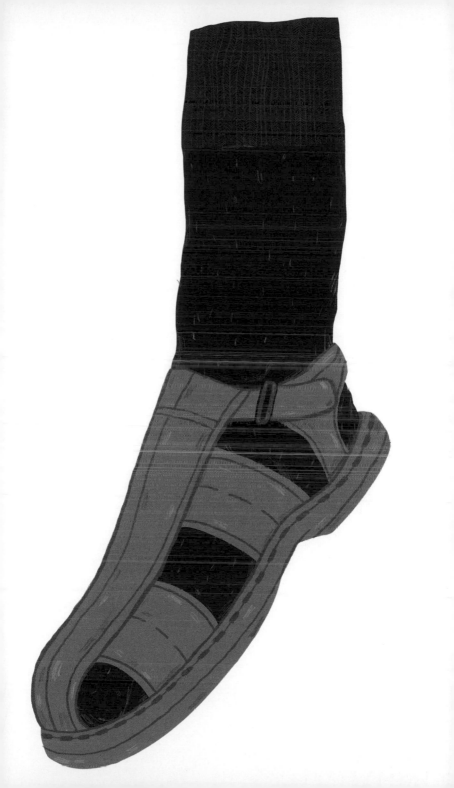

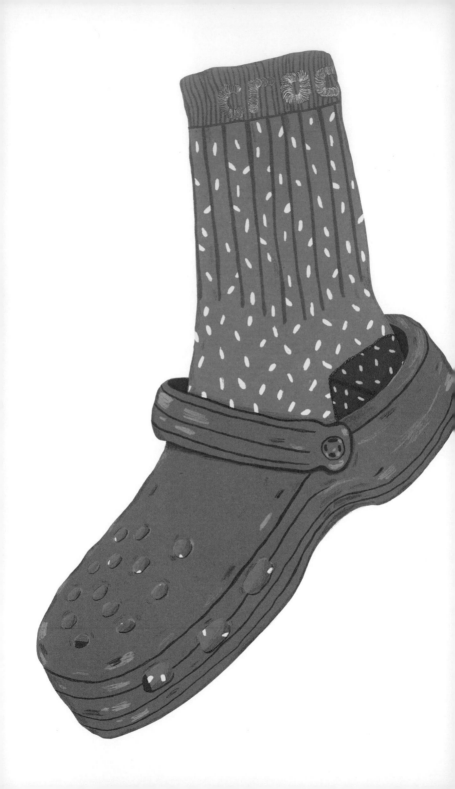

Socks with
Crocs

No.

Compression Socks

Likes to keep the blood flowing with a little squeeze. A hug to the calf is never in vein.

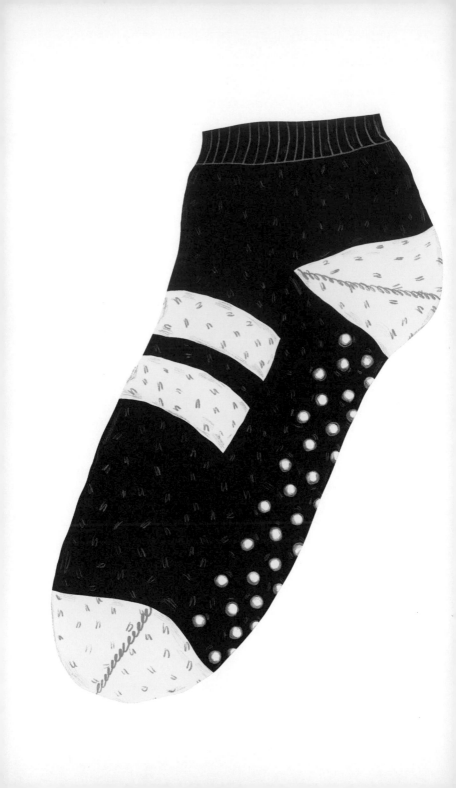

Yoga Socks

Knows that the best way to reach inner peace is by not face-planting on their mat during Warrior II pose. Namaste.

SOCKS LOOKING FOR A MATE

Low-Rise Sock

9 1 Mile Away

"I work hard and play harder.

LIKES: Toes.

DISLIKES: Walks on the beach but only because of the sand.

Are you my perfect match?"

Lonely Dress Sock

9 15 Miles Away

"I like my partners like I like my coffee. Swipe right if you're full-flavored, no nonsense, and ready to knock me off my foot."

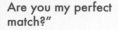

Novelty Sock Looking for a Mate

9 *3 Blocks Away*

"Could you be my sole-mate? I'm a whimsical and crazy sock, ready to get wild together. Be my plus one."

Single White Tube Sock Seeks Same

9 *20 Miles Away*

"**YOU:** Not afraid to take a risk and go above midcalf.

ME: Unraveled by your beauty.

Let's pair up, baby."

Hopeless Romantic Sock

9 *Behind the Dryer*

"I know you're out there, and I won't stop looking until I find you! Without you, there's a hole in my heart. And also in my toe."

Spats

Upon seeing these decorative sock-like non-socks worn over shoes, one wonders: Is this person a gangster from the early 1900s? Headed to a fancy dinner at Downton Abbey? Or maybe part of a marching band? Check for a tuba.

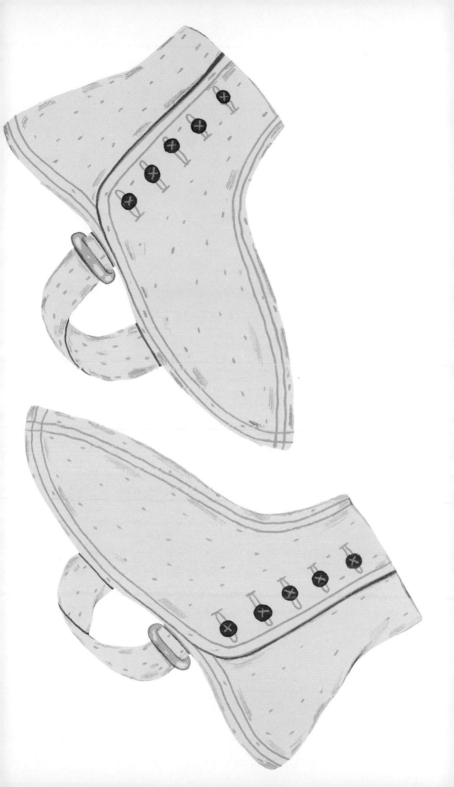

Army Socks

Ready for any situation. Tromping through the desert, parachuting out of a helicopter, or marching in formation. Sound off: One-two-three-four, one-two, THREE-FOUR!

Bobby Socks

All dressed up for the sock hop with
nowhere to go since it's not 1950.
Guess they'll just have to hang out at
the malt shop with Fonzie. Ayyyy.

Pom-Pom Socks

Likes a peppy flair around the Achilles tendon. Rah rah, siss boom bah!
Gooo team!

Stocking-Stuffer Socks

Obviously this person is related to someone who was desperately buying a gift at the last minute. But they're not mad about it. Reindeer rock.

I Want Your Socks
Let's Talk about Socks, Baby
Despasockto
Socks on Fire
We Will Sock You
You Socked Me All Night Long
Sock Me Amadeus
All the Single Sockies

PLAYLIST

NOISE HIGH OUTPUT

B:

Handmade Socks

Wearable proof that this person is loved. It took someone four weeks to stitch these babies, so they need to be appreciated. And not just because the person that made them is holding sharp knitting needles.

Grippy Socks

Cautious, careful, doesn't want any slip-ups.
This is a truly grounded person. Mostly
because they're stuck to the ground.

Cashmere Socks

A lover of luxury. A person of style. Believes that their feet deserve the champagne of socks. Cheers!

Leg Warmers

Still loves the '80s. Hey, you never know
when an aerobics class might break out.

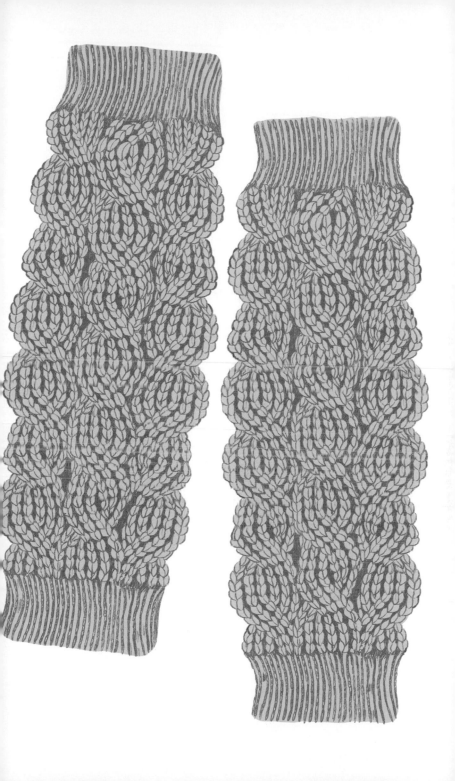

Superfan Socks

Loves *Star Wars*, *Star Trek*, and Marvel, especially on their feet. The Force is strong with this one.

NEW CONCEPTS IN SOCKS!

It's the twenty-first century, and that means it's time to DISRUPT SOCKS. This ain't your parents' sock drawer, bro. It's time for a MAJOR REFRESH of the cotton fabric that covers your TOES. Get your feet ready for these NEW CONCEPTS IN SOCKS!

STOCKS

Socks made out of old dollar bills, which are worthless in today's cashless society. Buy low, sell high, get rich with these Washingtons. (Note: Can also be used to pay for cigarettes in a pinch.)

SHOCKS

Remember when you were a kid and you'd run around the carpet in your socks building static electricity to shock your sister? Our new shocks take that to the next level! Each shock is outfitted with mini electrical wires. One sprint across the carpet and you'll be sparking like a casino sign!

SPOCKS

People love *Star Trek*. That's why we created these badass socks that look like the human-Vulcan Spock, with side pockets shaped like his famous pointy ears. The perfect sock for staying in and not having a date. Again.

CROCKS

You might have heard that it's lame to wear socks and Crocs, but know what isn't lame? Socks attached to unfashionable plastic slip-on shoes: a.k.a. Crocks! Save yourself the exhausting hassle of putting on a sock, and then putting on a Croc, with this new look that cuts out the middleman. Sexy? Oh, hell yes.

Thermal Socks

Q: Why is this a great person to marry?
A: Because they'll never get cold feet.

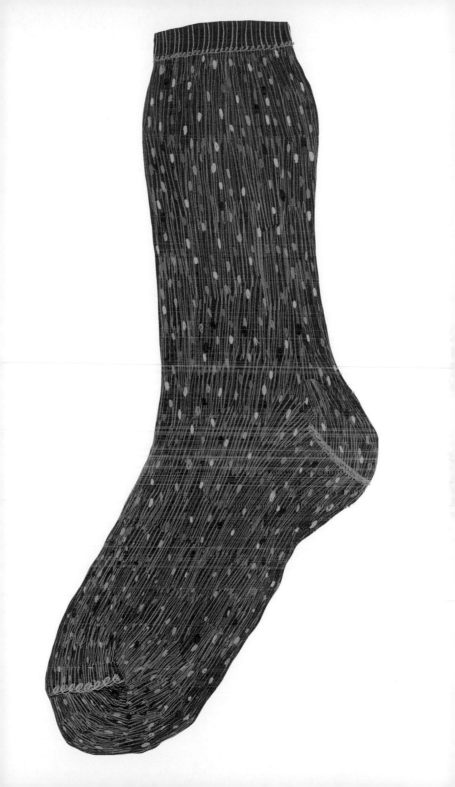

Character Socks

Perhaps this person seems professional.
Maybe you think they're well-dressed.
Until you look a little lower.
Then it's SpongeBob time.

Socks
Printed with
Pet Photos

We've all seen the Instagram ads.
This person just couldn't resist bringing
their pet everywhere.

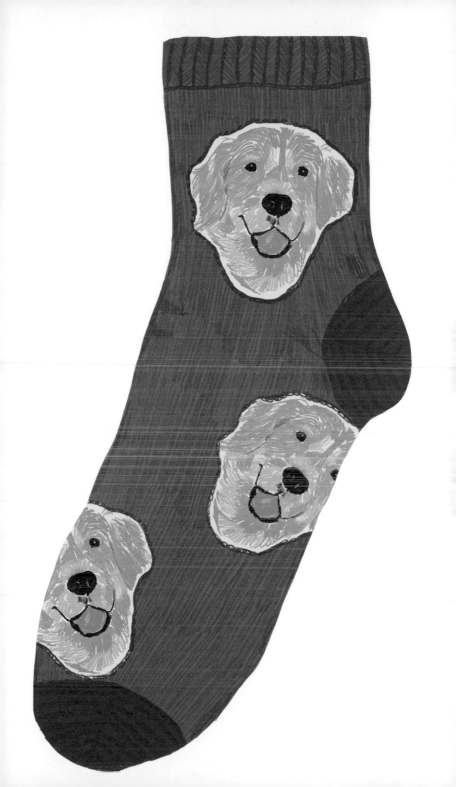

Rainbow
Socks

It may be cloudy outside, but it's always a beautiful day on this optimistic person's feet. Follow them to the nearest juice bar.

Hiking Socks

Embraces nature. But not blisters. Which is why they need socks that can go the distance even when their feet want to quit.

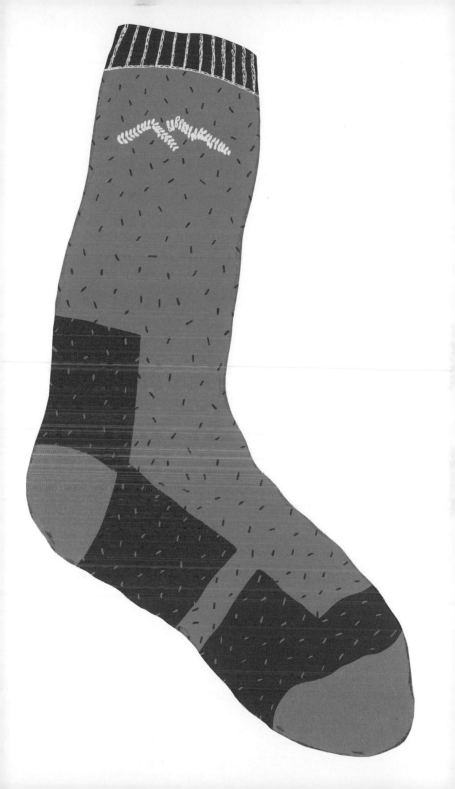

THE SOCK MONKEY SPEAKS

Yo, it's me. Sock Monkey. You know, the famous children's toy made out of a sock. Yep. That's right. A frickin' sock. I could have been made of plastic, or wood, or platinum, or even Swarovski crystals, but nope. I exist because some lazy-ass toymaker was inspired to create whimsical fun when he looked down at his own foot.

I'm not bitter, though. Not even about the fact that I could have been a sock dragon. That would have been amazing. I would rule the toy box. Lego and baby dolls and blocks would make me their leader. "All bow down to Sock Dragon!" But that will never happen because the toymaker shoved a bunch of stuffing inside me and said, "Look! A monkey!" and forever doomed me to the life of a jester of the play-room. Nobody takes me seriously. They never have. Especially those asshole army men who make me play Monkey in the Middle. But how could they respect me with this idiotic, big red yarn smile of mine? With this lame pom-pom hat? I'd punch my own self out if I had any upper arm strength.

Oh, and another thing: Unlike every other toy, I don't want to become real like Pinocchio. I mean, become a real sock? Spend my life inside some poor schmo's shoe? No, thank you. Imagine the smell. [Shudder.]

But wait a second—maybe I'd become a real monkey! Then I could move to Costa Rica or some other place that has a rainforest, and I'd eat bananas and climb trees and meet other monkeys and get in monkey fights and maybe be eaten by a tiger and . . . you know what? Never mind. I'll just stay here in the toy box.

Socks with Bad Elastic That Really Need to Be Thrown Away

This person is not a quitter.
Unlike these crappy socks.

Midcalf Socks

Not too high, not too low. Their sweet spot is in the middle. Like Goldilocks. Or Midtown Manhattan.

Trampoline Park Socks

Always ready to jump into a good time.
Likes to fly high. Also appreciates a
good health code requirement.

Moisturizing Socks

Likes to be pampered at all times.
Who has the softest feet in town?
This smooth-toed operator, that's who.

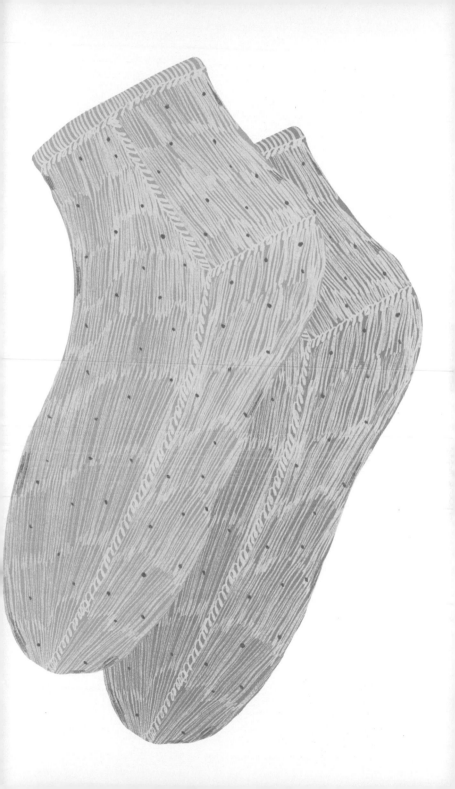

Hemp Socks

Always smokes 'em if they got 'em.
But never gets high on their own supply.
Meaning, this person will never go one toke,
or toe, over the line.

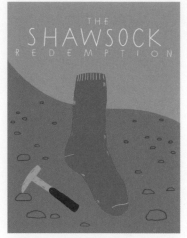

Two wrongly imprisoned socks bond in their drawer, and then escape to freedom when someone forgets to shut it.

A washed up sockstar begins dating a socksy singer, but when she soon steals the socklight, he continues to unravel.

Dorothy and her little dog Toe-Toe travel to meet the Wizard, who tells her to click her ruby red socks together three times.

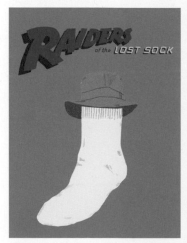

Famous archaeologist Indiana Jones must nab the Sock of the Covenant before the Nazis do!

HE MOVIES!

Luke Sockwalkor, Han Socklo, and Chewsocka use the Force to restore freedom in a galaxy far, far away.

"Socks ... find a way."

"I simply remember my favorite socks, and then I don't feel so bad."

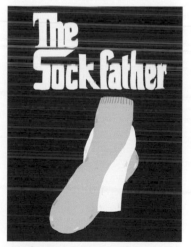

Mafia boss Vito Sockleone and his family try to run the family "accessories" business without getting whacked.

Now go
out and
rock those
socks!